Priscilla Ann **Presley**, née Wagner, changed by adoption to Beaulieu, born May 24th, 1945, Brooklyn, New York, U.S., is an actress and businesswoman. Married to Elvis Presley from 1967 to 1973, she served as chairwoman of Elvis Presley Enterprises (EPE), the company that turned Graceland into one of the top tourist attractions in the U. S. Priscilla had a starring role as Jane Spencer in the 3 Naked Gun movies, in which she co-starred with Leslie Nielsen, having also played the role of Jenna Wade on the long-running TV series Dallas.

Priscilla's maternal grandfather, Albert Henry Iversen, was born during 1899 in Egersund, Norway then migrated to the US, where he wed Lorraine, who was of Scots-Irish and English descent. Their only daughter, Anna Lillian Iversen, was born in March 1926, her name later being changed to Ann, before she gave birth to Priscilla when aged 19.

Her biological father was US Navy pilot James Wagner, son of Kathryn and Harold Wagner, having married Ann at the age of 23, after the couple had been dating for over 3 years. James was killed in a plane crash while returning home on leave when Priscilla was 6 months old. When she later discovered this "family secret" through clues in an old wooden box of family keepsakes, Ann encouraged her to keep the revelation from her half-siblings from her 2nd marriage, lest it "endanger our family closeness."

Ann Wagner met a United States Air Force officer named Paul Beaulieu, from Quebec, Canada during 1948, the couple getting wed within a year. Paul took over raising Priscilla, who announced his death on January 4th, 2018 on her social media accounts. She took his surname as Priscilla helped care for the growing family over the next few years, as his Air Force career took them from Connecticut to New Mexico, followed by Maine. Priscilla described herself during this period as "a shy, pretty, little girl, unhappily accustomed to moving from base to base every 2 or 3 years."

Priscilla later recalled how uneasy she felt having to move so often, never knowing if she could make friends, or if she'd fit in with the people she'd meet at the next place. The Beaulieus settled in Del Valle, Texas in 1956, but her stepfather was soon transferred to Wiesbaden, Germany. Priscilla was "crushed" by this news, coming just after junior high, fearful of having to leave friends behind then make new ones.

When the Beaulieus arrived in Germany, they stayed at the Helene Hotel but after 3 months, living there became too expensive, so they looked for a place to rent. The family settled into a large apartment in a "vintage building, constructed long before World War I," but soon after moving in, they realized it was a brothel, although given the scarcity of housing, they had little choice but to remain.

Elvis Presley met Priscilla during his Army career, on September 13th, 1959, when attending a party at his home in Bad Nauheim, West Germany. Although only 14 years old, she made a huge impression on him, Elvis being said to have acted like an "awkward, embarrassed" boy-next-door figure in front of her but managed to compose himself by the end of the evening.

Priscilla's parents were upset by her late return home on the night of that first meeting, demanding that she never see Presley again but his keenness for another rendezvous, along with his promise never to bring her home late again led them to relent. Thereafter, Elvis and Priscilla were often together until he left West Germany, during March 1960.

Following his departure, Priscilla was inundated with requests for interviews from media outlets around the world, having received mail from Elvis fans, as well as letters from "lonesome G.I.s". Due to gossip-magazine rumours about his relationship with Nancy Sinatra, Priscilla became convinced that her romance with Presley was over, believing she'd never see him again.

After his return to the US, she stayed in touch with Elvis by phone, although they didn't see each other again until the summer of 1962, when Priscilla's parents let her visit for a fortnight. They allowed her to go on the condition that Presley pay for a first-class round trip, while arranging for her to be chaperoned at all times, insisting that she write home every day. Elvis agreed to all their demands, so Priscilla flew to Los Angeles. Presley told her they were going to Las Vegas then had Priscilla pre-write a postcard for every day they'd be away, being mailed from Los Angeles by a member of his staff.

While on the trip to Las Vegas, Priscilla first took amphetamines and sleeping pills to keep up with the lifestyle of Elvis. Following another visit at Christmas, her parents let her move to Memphis permanently in March 1963, after Presley agreed that Priscilla would attend an all-girls Catholic school, the Immaculate Conception High School in Memphis, Tennessee, while living with Elvis's father and his stepmother in a house a few streets away from his Graceland mansion, on Hermitage Drive 3650, until she graduated from high school during June 1963.

However, Priscilla stated in her autobiography, Elvis and Me (1985) that she "spent entire nights with Grandma at Graceland and gradually moved her belongings there". It's believed that she had her permanent residence at Graceland by early May 1963, her parents eventually agreeing to her living there if Presley promised to marry her. Priscilla later said, "The move was natural. I was there all the time anyway."

Priscilla was keen to go to Hollywood with Elvis, but he kept telling her that he was too busy, having had her stay in Memphis. Presley began an affair with his co-star Ann-Margret during the filming of Viva Las Vegas, Priscilla confronting him when she read the reports in the press. Elvis told her that they were simply rumours to promote the movie and that she shouldn't believe everything that she read in the press. Presley had intimate relationships with many of his leading ladies and co-stars over the next few years, denying their existence to Priscilla, who was allowed to visit him in Hollywood eventually, but her visits were kept short.

Elvis proposed to Priscilla shortly before Christmas 1966, accounts suggesting that she threatened to take her story to the press if Presley refused to marry her, and that her father threatened to have Elvis charged under the Mann Act; "taking a minor across state lines for sexual purposes". Colonel Parker, Presley's manager, also encouraged him to marry by reminding him about his RCA "morals clause" within his record contract.

Priscilla suggested in an interview with Ladies' Home Journal that she and Elvis were quite happy to just live together, but "at that time it wasn't nice for people to live together". Presley's cook, Alberta, said that he was so upset about the wedding that she caught him crying about it one day. When she asked why

Elvis didn't just cancel the wedding if it upset him so much, he replied "I don't have a choice." Marty Lacker, a close friend of Presley, also spoke about his reluctance to marry, while others including Joe Esposito, have stated that Elvis was excited to marry Priscilla.

Priscilla described Presley in her book, Elvis and Me, as a very passionate man who wasn't overtly sexual towards her, stating that he told her that they had to wait until they were married before having intercourse. Presley said, "I'm not saying we can't do other things. It's just the actual encounter. I want to save it." Priscilla said in her autobiography that she was a virgin, she and Elvis not having sex until their wedding night but this was questioned by biographer Suzanne Finstad.

The couple married on May 1st, 1967, at the Aladdin Hotel in Las Vegas, the wedding, arranged by Parker to maximize publicity, having had very few guests, being over in only 8 minutes. It was followed by a short press conference and a $10,000 breakfast reception, attended by friends, family, and business associates from MGM, RCA, and the William Morris Agency.

The wedding led to rifts between Presley and several of his closest friends who weren't invited to the ceremony, Red West being particularly furious. He and his wife had been personally invited by Elvis to Las Vegas for the wedding, having been dressed for the occasion, but at the last minute were told that they wouldn't be present.

For Red, who'd been with Presley since the start of his rise to fame, Elvis having been best man at his wedding, it was a big enough insult that he quit his job working for Presley. Many of his other friends were also disappointed, having harboured resentment towards him for many years to follow, although they mostly blamed Colonel Parker for their exclusion rather than Elvis himself.

Following the reception, the couple boarded a private jet flying them to a short honeymoon in Palm Springs. They flew back to Memphis on May 4th, retreating to their private ranch, just over the Mississippi state line, for a 3-week break, where many of Presley's' inner circle joined them, although for the most part the pair were left alone to enjoy each other's company without the intrusion of the Memphis Mafia.

Priscilla reveled in her chance to be a proper wife, cooking, cleaning, and washing for her husband, later saying, "I loved playing house. Here was an opportunity to take care of him myself. No maids or housekeepers to pamper us." Trying to heal rifts, Elvis and Priscilla held another reception at Graceland on May 29th for the friends and family who weren't able to attend the original ceremony.

Shortly afterwards, Priscilla discovered that she was pregnant, being upset at such an early pregnancy, sure that it would destroy the closeness between them, having asked him earlier if she could take birth control pills, but Presley had insisted that they weren't perfected yet. She considered abortion, discussing it with Elvis, but both decided that they couldn't live with themselves if they went through with it. Their only child, Lisa Marie, was born exactly 9 months after their wedding, on February 1st, 1968.

Priscilla wrote in Elvis and Me that at around the time Presley was filming Live a Little, Love a Little (1968), she began taking private dance lessons, becoming strongly attracted to the instructor, known as Mark in the book, confessing to having a short affair, saying, "I came out of it realizing that I needed much more out of my relationship with Elvis."

Despite Priscilla's affair and Presley's relationships with his co-stars, the first few years of their marriage seemed a happy time for the couple. However, when his musical career took off again after his TV special during 1968, he was constantly touring and playing in Las Vegas. Elvis had also been seeing other women on and off, often leaving Priscilla at home with Lisa Marie, being away so often that their marriage soured.

Presley was a keen karate student, persuading Priscilla to take it up, who thought it was a good idea, as it would help pass the time she spent alone if she had a hobby on which to concentrate, also being keen to share in his interests. Priscilla began taking lessons from Mike Stone, a karate instructor she'd met backstage at one of Elvis' concerts in 1972, soon beginning an affair with him.

Priscilla stated in her book, "My relationship with Mike had now developed into an affair. I still loved Elvis deeply, but over the next few months I knew I'd have to make a crucial decision regarding my destiny. Elvis must've perceived my new restlessness." A couple of months later, she said that Presley had asked to see her in his hotel suite, where she wrote in her book that Elvis "forcefully made love to me... saying, 'This is how a real man makes love to his woman.'"

Priscilla later stated in an interview that she regretted her choice of words in describing the incident, saying that it had been an overstatement. She went on to say that following the incident, "what really hurt was that he was not sensitive to me as a woman and his attempt at reconciliation had come too late," suggesting that Presley's actions were compensation for his lack of sexual interest in her, which had been a source of hurt and discontent to her for years.

Priscilla stated in her book: "He'd mentioned to me before we were married that he'd never been able to make love to a woman who had a child", later expressing the personal repercussions of their sexual dysfunction: "I'm beginning to doubt my own sexuality as a woman. My physical and emotional needs were unfulfilled." After the incident, Priscilla wrote: "this was not the gentle, understanding man I grew to love."

Elvis and Priscilla separated on February 23rd, 1972 then filed for legal separation on July 26th. To avoid Priscilla's having to make her home address available on the public records, risking the security of her and Lisa Marie, Presley filed for divorce on his 38th birthday, January 8th, 1973. Later that month, Elvis apparently became paranoid about Stone, having said: "There's too much pain in me... Stone [must] die."

Presley's outbursts continued with such intensity that a doctor wasn't able to calm him, despite large doses of medication. After another two days of raging, his friend and bodyguard, Red West, made enquiries about arranging a contract killing of Stone, but was relieved when Elvis said, "Aw hell, let's just leave it for now. Maybe it's a bit heavy." The divorce was finalized on October 9th, 1973.

The couple agreed to share custody of their daughter, Priscilla being awarded an outright cash payment of $725,000, as well as spousal support, child support, 5% of Presley's new publishing companies and half the income from the sale of their Beverly Hills home. Originally the couple had agreed upon a much smaller settlement; a $100,000 lump payment, $1,000 / month spousal support, and $500 / month child support, Priscilla being keen to make it on her own to prove that her marriage to Elvis hadn't been about money. However, soon afterwards, her new lawyers persuaded her to increase her demands, arguing that a star of Presley's stature could easily afford more for his ex-wife and child. Priscilla and Elvis remained close, leaving the courthouse on the day of their divorce hand in hand.

Following her split from Presley, she set up a joint venture with her friend and stylist Olivia Bis during 1973, the pair opening a clothing boutique in Los Angeles called Bis & Beau. Elvis was supportive of Priscilla's venture, contacting several friends in public relations to help with promotion for the launch. In an interview that year to promote the opening of the store, Priscilla said, "After the separation, I had to make up my mind about what I wanted to do, and since I'd worked with Olivia for such a long time on my own clothes, I decided to try it professionally. We both do the designing for the shop, and have people who sew for us." The boutique was a successful venture, with celebrity clients including Cher, Lana Turner, Barbra Streisand, and Natalie Wood shopping there regularly before it closed in 1976.

After Presley's death on August 16th the following year, Priscilla acted as executor for his only heir, their daughter, Lisa Marie, who was only aged 9. Graceland cost $500,000 / year in upkeep, with expenses and taxes due on the property having led Lisa Marie's inheritance to dwindle to only $1 million. Faced with having to sell Graceland, Priscilla examined other famous homes/museums, hiring a CEO, Jack Soden, to turn Graceland into a tourist attraction, being opened to the public on June 7th, 1982.

Only 4 weeks after opening Graceland's doors, the estate had made back all the money it had invested. Priscilla became the chairwoman and president of Elvis Presley Enterprises (EPE), stating that she'd remain in the post until Lisa Marie reached 21 years of age. Under Priscilla's guidance, the enterprise's fortunes soaring, the trust growing to be worth over $100 million.

Priscilla launched her own range of fragrances during 1988, following it up with a range of linen, having also helped to produce a couple of movies, including Breakfast with Einstein and Finding Graceland. Priscilla was elected to the board of directors at Metro-Goldwyn-Mayer in September 2000 then became the executive producer of a 14-track album titled If I Can Dream: Elvis Presley With the Royal Philharmonic Orchestra during 2015. She stated "If Elvis were here, he'd be evolving and taking risks, seemingly like everybody else today."

That year the U.S. Postmaster General, Megan Brennan, and Priscilla dedicated an Elvis "forever" stamp, which featured a black and white shot by photographer William Speer from 1955. It was her 2nd dedication of a USPS stamp. The first Elvis stamp, issued in 1993, was the most popular edition of stamps in the Postal Service history. Presley became the first musical artist to be featured on 2 different collections of stamps.

Hal B. Wallis, a Hollywood producer who'd financed many of Presley's earlier films, had shown an interest in signing Priscilla to a contract. However, Elvis had no intention of allowing his wife to have a career of any kind, believing that, "a woman's place was in the home looking after her man". Priscilla had shown an interest in dancing and modeling, but Presley's views led her to keep them as hobbies instead of pursuing them as careers, having had the opportunity to model for a local store once, but when Elvis heard about it, he asked her to give it up.

Priscilla was offered the role of one of Charlie's Angels but turned it down because she didn't like the show, before making her TV debut as co-host of Those Amazing Animals during 1980. Priscilla got her first chance to act professionally on a season 2 episode of The Fall Guy, titled "Manhunter" in 1983. She was then cast in a role in a TV movie titled Love is Forever, starring alongside Michael Landon.

Although Priscilla was treated well by most of the cast and crew, with her acting being praised by several of her co-stars, she found Landon difficult to work with on set. After the TV film was broadcast, Priscilla was given the role of Jenna Wade in the soap opera Dallas. She was the third actress to play the role of Jenna, having played it for the longest, leaving the show during 1988 after 5 years.

Priscilla starred opposite Leslie Nielsen that year in The Naked Gun: From the Files of Police Squad! as Jane Spencer, going on to act in the next 2 films in the series: The Naked Gun 2 1/2: The Smell of Fear (1991) and Naked Gun 33 1/3: The Final Insult (1994). She made guest appearances on a number of TV series in the late '90s, including Melrose Place, Touched by an Angel, and Spin City. Priscilla made her pantomime debut in Snow White and the Seven Dwarfs at the New Wimbledon Theatre, Wimbledon, London, during the Christmas of 2012, starring opposite Warwick Davis.

She's been the Ambassador of the Dream Foundation since 2003, a Santa Barbara-based wish-granting organization for terminally ill adults and their families. Reports in the media in October 2017 that Priscilla had left the Church of Scientology were refuted by her. She spoke out against the Tennessee Ag-Gag Bill during 2013, in a letter to Tennessee Governor Bill Haslam, citing her and Presley's love of horses, expressing her concern that the bill would hinder animal cruelty investigations, while reducing protection of horses and other farm animals.

Priscilla's longest relationship has been with Marco Garibaldi, whom she lived with for 22 years. Their son, Navarone, was born on March 1st, 1987 when she was starring in the primetime soap opera Dallas, her pregnancy being written into the storyline. The couple ended their relationship in 2006.

Priscilla had a square named after her in Egersund, Norway: Priscilla Presleys plass, on the street where her grandfather was born and lived. The opening ceremony took place on August 23rd, 2008.

Filmography

Year	Title	Role	Notes
1983	Love Is Forever	Sandy Redford	TV film

Year	Title	Role	Notes
1983	The Fall Guy	Sabrina Coldwell	Episode: "Manhunter"
1983–88	Dallas	Jenna Wade	Series regular, 143 episodes

Soap Opera Digest Award for New Actress in a Prime Time Soap Opera (1984)

Year	Title	Role	Notes
1988	The Naked Gun: From the Files of Police Squad!	Jane Spencer	
1990	The Adventures of Ford Fairlane	Colleen Sutton	
1991	The Naked Gun 2½: The Smell of Fear	Jane Spencer	nominated — MTV Movie Award for Best Kiss
1993	Tales from the Crypt	Gina	Episode: "Oil's Well That Ends Well"
1994	Naked Gun 33⅓: The Final Insult	Jane Spencer Drebin	
1996	Melrose Place	Nurse Benson	Episodes: "Peter's Excellent Adventure" "Full Metal Betsy" "Dead Sisters Walking"
1997	Touched by an Angel	Dr. Meg Saulter	Episode: "Labor of Love"
1998	Breakfast with Einstein	Keelin	TV film
1999	Spin City	Aunt Marie Paterno	Episodes: "Dick Clark's Rockin' Make-Out Party '99" and "Back to the Future IV: Judgment Day."

1999   Hayley Wagner, Star   Sue Wagner TV film

2019   Wedding at Graceland   Priscilla Presley TV film

Bibliography

Presley, Priscilla (1985). Elvis and Me. ISBN 0-399-12984-7.

Presley, Priscilla; Presley, Lisa Marie (2005). Elvis by the Presleys. ISBN 0-307-23741-9.

Further reading

Clayton, Rose / Dick Heard (2003). Elvis: By Those Who Knew Him Best. Virgin Publishing Limited. ISBN 0-7535-0835-4.

Clutton, Helen (2004). Everything Elvis. ISBN 0-7535-0960-1.

Edwards, Michael (1988). Priscilla, Elvis and Me. ISBN 0312022689.

Finstad, Suzanne (1997). Child Bride: The Untold Story of Priscilla Beaulieu Presley.

Goldman, Albert (1981). Elvis. ISBN 0-14-005965-2.

Guralnick, Peter (1999). Careless Love. The Unmaking of Elvis Presley. Back Bay Books. ISBN 0-316-33297-6.

Guralnick, Peter; Jorgensen, Ernst (1999). Elvis: Day by Day. ISBN 0-345-42089-6.

Priscilla wed Elvis on May 1st, 1967, in Las Vegas, Nev., when she was 21 & he was 32, following a 7-year romance. Presley was earning $4 million / yr as an actor-singer. The couple had a daughter, Lisa Marie on February 1st, 1968 then the couple separated during August, 1972, Elvis filing for divorce the following year, giving Priscilla custody of their daughter. As they waited for the divorce to become final, Elvis lived in the $550,000 Holmby Hills estate he once shared with his wife, while Priscilla and Lisa lived in a large, 5-room penthouse apartment overlooking a small marina on the Pacific Palisades.

When Priscilla was aged 10, her father, Captain Beaulieu, was transferred to Austin, Tex. then 4 years later the family moved to his new post in Weisbaden, West Germany, not far from Bad Nauheim, where draftee Elvis Presley was serving in the United States Army's 3rd Armored Division. It was there that Sgt. Presley 25, met Priscilla, 14.

The the Pacific Palisades apartment décor was sheer and soft, with billowy organdy curtains and calico sofas, there being a conspicuous lack of anything masculine. There wasn't a photograph or a memento in view to suggest that Priscilla had been the wife of Elvis Presley. The smell of jasmine wafted into the living room as she entered from the kitchen carrying a tea tray, standing 5 ft, 2 ins tall, weighing 110 lbs, being stylishy dressed in a splashy, purple print blouse and pants. More impressive than who she was or what she was wearing was her aristocratic bearing, everything about her suggesting grace and poise. Priscilla was beautiful, perhaps the most beautifully kept secret in Hollywood, as outside the inner circle of Presley's friends, few people knew what his wife really looked like.

Priscilla handled herself with ease and confidence, saying as she poured tea that she was reluctant to talk about her life with Elvis, her desire to protect her own privacy being as strong as her impulse to shelter him, having guarded her life with Presley since she'd first met him. Even before she got to Germany, Priscilla had thought about what it would be like to meet Elvis:

"I didn't have great fantasies about meeting him but I do remember that when my father told us he was being sent to Weisbaden Air Base, I mentioned jokingly that Elvis was stationed nearby and maybe we'd get a chance to meet him. My mother said 'I wouldn't let you walk across the street to see Elvis Presley', which seems funny now, doesn't it?"

Then, a week and a half after I got to Germany, I was eating in a little place where most of the military kids went, when a guy asked if I wanted to meet Elvis Presley. I said, 'Fine' thinking it was all a joke. For my so-called date with Elvis, I didn't dress up; I just wore a little sailor dress, because I still didn't believe it but the next thing I knew I was on my way to his house, which he shared with his father, Vernon Presley'.

3 or 4 of his friends were with their dates, and a couple of girls dropped by. It was a very casual evening - a family atmosphere. Elvis was sitting in a chair when I arrived, before he got up to shake my hand. Then reality hit me, and I thought, 'What am I doing here?" Priscilla recalled that her parents were waiting up when she got home. "They asked me how it was, and I told them exactly what had happened: that Elvis was very nice and warm and cordial, but that I never thought I'd see him again. Then he called.

At first, my parents said that I shouldn't date Elvis, that I was too young, which was true but my mother felt that it was a once-in-a-lifetime opportunity and besides, it wasn't harming me". Finally she prevailed upon Dad to allow it but he set up a 12 o'clock curfew. "Each date with Elvis was the same. Usually he'd have his father pick me up in a car. Elvis' mother [Gladys Presley] had died in 1958. In Germany, Vernon was dating a pretty blonde named Devanda 'Dee' Elliot. Sometimes they'd join us and some friends for a movie or something.

No, I was never impressed with dating Elvis. Perhaps I thought that it was all a dream, or maybe it was because Elvis was very down to earth. He made me comfortable. Elvis fit in with everybody, too. Elvis wasn't aggressive with me, he never pushed. He was very gentle". Priscilla was reluctant to go into detail, saying that their romance blossomed steadily.

One of her outstanding qualities was her sensitivity to Presley, never breathing a word to anyone during the whole time she dated him. When asked why, she said, "Oh, there were many possible reasons. I felt that he was publicized so much already; it was my own life, my own business, or maybe it was because Elvis is so self-protective. He's his own man, a very understanding, compassionate person, and he accepts people fully but as far as his personal life's concerned, he's very secretive".

Her intuitive sense about Presley might be how the relationship survived after he left Germany. 'When Elvis was discharged from the Army, I was still in Wiesbaden. I had no idea that I'd ever see him again. I was dumbfounded when he asked me to spend Christmas in Memphis - and then he asked if I could remain there. Of course, my Mum and Dad said definitely, no but Elvis called then talked to them, so I finished my senior year at the Immaculate Conception High School in Memphis".

During her stay in Memphis, Priscilla lived with Vernon and Dee, who had since married, with Devanda's 3 young sons, in the east wing of the Presley's famed estate, Graceland. Vernon and Dee looked after Priscilla, helping her to adjust to the kind of life in a fishbowl that she'd be leading. Although she and Presley never talked of marriage, Priscilla - or Cilla, as Elvis called her - never felt awkward about the situation:

"First of all, Elvis wouldn't have asked me to come if there wasn't a reason. I believed that he cared for me, and that he wouldn't have taken the responsibility of pulling me out of school and putting me into another if he wasn't making some commitment. Anyway, he's not the kind of person to take advantage of anybody, so I felt very secure. As I said, I had no idea that we were going to be married, but I had faith that things would handle themselves. I didn't think that I'd be deserted or neglected at any time, because Elvis had assured my parents that no harm would come to me".

During her 4-year stay, Priscilla led a Cinderella existence, her every dream having become a reality. When he was home, Presley tried to make up for the time he'd been away; he gave her little presents: "It was difficult for Elvis to buy for me, and a lot times he would just tell me to get what I wanted, which I liked. He gave me all of the cars that I've had. We started out with a little red Corvair, then a Chevrolet, a Toronado, an Eldorado then the Mercedes, a white one, which I drive now". When she wasn't driving her own car, Presley chauffeured her in a Lincoln Continental, equipped with a little TV and a bar. "It only served soft drinks, because Elvis doesn't drink or smoke.

Well, recently I think he's begun to smoke a pipe. We had a day cook and a night cook, who prepared simple American food.

Elvis would rent an entire cinema, invite friends then we'd talk loudly to each other without worrying that the manager would throw us out. Elvis loved good, action-packed movies, some Westerns and he loved A Shot in the Dark with Peter Sellers. No, Elvis never showed his own movies. He just preferred not to see them. Maybe he didn't say a line right or he thought that his hair didn't look good, or that he appeared fat. He just didn't want to see himself. He's very self-critical".

Priscilla would visit Presley in Hollywood occasionally, but she was careful to stay away from the set when he was shooting. "I didn't think that he could do his best if I was around. I felt that was his job, his business, so it wasn't my place to be there. Most of the time I stayed in Memphis, occupying my time at the dance studio, or went to dinner with a girl friend. I was perfectly happy the way it was".

Priscilla took a self-improvement course at the Patricia Stevens Finishing School, stressing that it wasn't to compete with Elvis' starlet friends, although confiding that it made her feel better to learn how to apply makeup. Yet when she thought back on it, she was amused. "When I went to Patricia Stevens I overdid it with makeup, because at that time I was going through the Cleopatra stage but it was fun. I still love to fool around with cosmetics, but not as much as when I was younger. I think every girl goes through that stage. How attractive I thought I looked at the time! Now when I see those old pictures of me with all that makeup on I think, 'Oh, how blind I was!'

I wish that Elvis had said something but he must've liked it, because he never commented. I do think that men in show business like to have women in makeup, because they're used to seeing women looking the best that they possibly can. Yet, I don't think it's changed Elvis' impression of me - I was always a little girl to him". Priscilla's makeup was as flawless as a model's, a light base and natural highlights complementing her fragile, fawnlike beauty but her new, natural look involved more than a makeup change. "The change is from being the person that you think you are, to accepting the person that you really are. I know who I am, where I stand, and I feel as if I have an identity; I don't have to be or please anybody other than myself".

For years Elvis and Priscilla had seemed happy not to marry, before in what seemed an overnight decision, they were wed on May 1st, 1967, in a double ring ceremony at the Las Vegas Aladdin Hotel. Priscilla wore a gown of white organza, trimmed in seed pearls with lace sleeves and a full train. A 3/4 length tulle veil was held by a crown of rhinestones.

Her wedding-engagement ring was a 3-carat diamond, surrounded by 20 smaller diamonds. Only 14 guests attended the wedding, including Dee, Vernon and the Beaulieus. "As a wedding present, Elvis flew in my mum and dad from his new post at Fort Ord, California. I remember how overwhelmed they were, how happy, too. Of course, they thought it was about time, as we'd been dating for years! Although many people thought our wedding was sudden, Elvis and I had been talking about it in stages. One day he showed me the ring then simply asked me to marry him. Even though we were perfectly content the way we were, at that time it wasn't nice for people to live together".

After a two month honeymoon in Palm Springs, Calif., the couple returned to their $400,000 mansion in the Trousdale Estates. Presley had just finished the film Double Trouble, being about to start another movie on location, so the first days of their marriage had a hit-and-run lifestyle that was to become their way of life. Priscilla didn't complain about it, saying:

"For Elvis to come home from a trip then leave again was routine. At first I wanted to go along and it was difficult for me to understand why I couldn't. Sure I was disappointed, but I got over it. The times that Elvis couldn't make an anniversary became a way of life. I may've been hurt, but it's an adjustment that you make as a wife. I kept thinking. 'It's going to work itself out - We'll make it somehow!' I had to, because if you think 'I'm always going to be alone', you'll go crazy. You have to live one day at a time, hoping that things aren't always going to be like that.

It was an adjustment, but I kept busy. I began studying karate. I won my green belt and was ready to test for my brown belt when I decided to drop out. I felt karate wasn't very feminine. So I decided to go back into ballet. I'd studied ballet years before with a woman named Maylee Kaplan. I enrolled again in her dance company; I stayed for c. 3 1/2 years. I danced and worked out every day and did a couple of recitals with them. Elvis didn't mind, so long as I was happy".

The birth of Lisa Marie was a blessing. Not only did it provide the Presleys with a much wanted child, but the baby gave Priscilla a new outlet for her energies, a love with whom she could spend her days. "Elvis and I were ecstatic over the birth of our daughter. If the baby had been a boy, we were going to name him John Barron. I liked the name Barron. It has a very strong feeling to it but when it was a girl, we decided on Lisa Marie - for no special reason, only because it's a very feminine name. She definitely has her father's eyes, but she has my features and petiteness. You know, the movie magazines have had me having about 5 miscarriages; I've never had a miscarriage.

When the baby got a little older I started going out more with other women whose husbands were in Elvis' group; we'd go to the park, go shopping, or go out for lunch. If Elvis got time off, we'd take a trip, but we were seldom by ourselves. For instance, our stay in Hawaii was supposed to be a cozy family vacation. Elvis had finished filming Blue Hawaii, and he wanted to show me the islands. So we rented a bungalow with a private beach but with an entourage of 12 people (each guy and his wife), how intimate can you become? I accepted it, but occasionally if I became resentful, Elvis would tease me out of it".

Much of the time being Mrs. Elvis Presley filled Priscilla with pride. "I felt very flattered when people stared at me in public, at a restaurant or on an opening night. I guess I'd be less than honest if I didn't say I liked the attention. Yet I never invited it by going to posh places where people go to be seen. That wasn't what I wanted. Maybe Elvis had a lot to do with that because he never associated with movie people. He had always had his own friends from his hometown. I was very happy to see that he was entertaining those people but I was also worried about someone getting hurt or Elvis getting sued and things like that".

How could she be so objective? "Because I know what it is. I know exactly why Elvis is up there on that stage, and it goes beyond seeing him as a superstar. He's a human being, and I can sense when he's nervous or if he's not doing the song as well as he did it the time before. I didn't see Elvis as a superstar: I saw him as my husband".

When the Presleys moved into a $550,000 mansion in Holmby Hills, Elvis was on the road, so Priscilla decorated the house herself. Her favourite room was his den. "I did it the way he wanted it: antiques, very manly. For the fireplace, I searched everywhere for wrought-iron and irons with eagle heads, and I bought antiques from all over Beverly Hills. I got old books and beautiful antique bar stools, and a desk that was furnished with a telephone and intercom.

Elvis liked the room; he spent a lot of time there. The sofa was done in suede - brown suede. The game room was done all in suede, with pinball machines and a pool table. After all, you've got to do what a man likes. He's got to live in it, and he's not going to be happy with anything feminine, that's for sure. The kitchen was very country and the breakfast nook was pleated and wicker, which didn't bother Elvis". Involvement with the house and the joys of raising Lisa Marie still didn't fill the gap of days and weeks when Presley was away and Priscilla was by herself. "Someone once said in jest that I should see other men, simply as friends, and that it would take my mind off being alone but when you're married, you just don't date other men".

Although a career of her own might've saved their marriage, Elvis didn't encourage Priscilla to work. "It's untrue that we argued about it, or about my becoming an actress. It's funny how rumours get started. The dance studio also had drama classes, so I attended one class. Someone started the rumor that I wanted to be an actress, which actually had never entered my mind. I did get offers to be in motion pictures, and Elvis left that up to me but it could never be, especially with a little daughter. Besides, I could never live that life. I saw how Elvis had to be. I mean, so publicized. I could live my life and do what I wanted, but it wasn't possible for Elvis to do that, which was a shame'.

More time with Presley was a continual hope for Priscilla, but it wasn't to be. "In mid-1972 I finally realized that things weren't going to change and that we had completely separate lives". Priscilla stated that she simply had to face the fact that Elvis was what Elvis was, and she was as she was. Would she continue to put up with it? Her answer was no. Presley filed for divorce on January 8th, 1972. The previous August they'd separated, Priscilla having moved out of their Holmby Hills mansion but there were no recriminations, no hard feelings on either side.

Elvis knew that Priscilla was there if he needed her - if he was sick or in trouble. Priscilla said that she worried about Lisa Marie, tenaciously shielding her from publicity. "Lisa Marie is so sensitive that a harsh word crushes her, but happily, she seems to have adjusted to the separation of her father and myself". Priscilla enfolded Lisa's Raggedy Ann doll in her arms. "She thinks daddy is on a business trip, so it works out and Elvis is no absentee father. When he's on tour, he often calls her, and when he's in town, he sees her a lot. She spent last weekend with him, and I took her to watch him perform in Las Vegas for her birthday".

Priscilla took pride in saying that she'd enrolled her daughter in "a very exclusive academy where they speak French - and she's only 5! I've also been thinking about giving Lisa some religious background, and have been considering the religion of Science. Have you heard anything about it? I really don't know that much about the Church, but I plan to look into it. I want to see for myself if I like it. I want Lisa to have a religious foundation, and I feel that I need it, too. I was raised as a Catholic, but I don't really believe that that is the way for me. I think that everybody needs some kind of support though and I'd like to get into something different - a more realistic religion".

Despite the 5 large rooms, Priscilla ran her household single-handed. "It's nice not having to cook and serve yourself but sometimes it can be uncomfortable, because you don't feel like being waited on. I'm used to doing things myself. I don't have any servants here by choice; I don't need anyone to help me. As a matter of fact, I've put in a request for a larger apartment in this building, one with a third bedroom, so Lisa's friends can stay over - and, when my parents visit. I'd rather have them stay here than go to a hotel. Fortunately, a 3 bedroom apartment will be available in time for when mother comes this summer'. Priscilla's parents lived in New Jersey with their 5 other children: Donald 22, Jeffrey, 13, twins Tim and Tom, 10, and Michelle 18.

The Beaulieu's still liked Elvis very much and respected him. "There are no hostilities whatsoever. They feel, I think, that Elvis and I are grown, mature people and that we know exactly what we're doing. As long as I'!m happy, they don't worry. The same with Vernon and Dee. They've been so wonderful and understanding".

Probably the most positive thing about the breakup was Priscilla's new career. Sample dress sketches covered the coffee table, Priscilla gathering them up with a burst of enthusiasm. "They're from a new boutique I've just opened on Robertson Boulevard in Los Angeles. It's called Bis & Beau, for Olivia Bis and Priscilla Beaulieu. It's only been open for a few weeks now and I am amazed that we're doing so well.

Olivia used to make my clothes when I was with Elvis. She also designs for Suzanne Pleshette, Barbara Parkins, and Zsa Zsa Gabor. I discovered her a few years ago. She had the sweetest mother-and- daughter outfit in the window - a white pique and paisley print ensemble, which I bought for one of Elvis' Las Vegas openings. After that, Olivia and I worked together on all of my outfits; I'd think up some kooky creation then she'd fit it to a pattern.

After the separation, I had to make up my mind about what I wanted to do, and since I'd worked with Olivia for such a long time on my own clothes, I decided to try it professionally. We both do the designing for the shop, and have people who sew for us. The dresses are priced from $65 up, and they're all original and handmade. We have specialty gift things too, like these watchbands". She fetched an array of brightly coloured, swiss-embroidered gingham, plaid, and seersucker watchbands from the drawer of the dining room hutch. "They're called Mikibeau, a name I made up - it means nothing special, but sounded cute, I thought - and are part of today's costume look".

In her spare time, Priscilla thought a lot about life, men, and marriage. "When you've lived a kind of a sheltered life, you're a little hesitant about being out in the world with other men. It's an adjustment. I went through stages where I didn't want to go out but I'm dating someone now, which is very good, because I have a secure feeling. His name is Mike Stone, and he's Hawaiian-born. He's a black belt karate champion', she said.

Pricilla refused to compare Mike to Elvis, although she conceded that Mike was the kind of male to whom she was attracted. "He's very much of a man to me, and treats me like a woman. I'd never go with a guy who wasn't boss. I mean the man would definitely have to be the more dominant person'. His schedule is flexible, so we can do things together. We both enjoy riding, and have horses, which we keep at the stables in Huntington Beach. Mike had his horse here and I brought Domino, a gift from Elvis, up from Memphis'.

Priscilla insisted that there was no possibility of a reconciliation with Presley, but she said she had no intention of marrying Stone: "I really can't say for the future - I only know about today and how I feel - but I don't have any plans for marriage. I think that there can be a very good relationship between two people that marriage can ruin. In marriage, you can easily take each other for granted. You begin to feel obligated.

I see it happening to my friends - every one is divorced - and I saw it happen to me. It's a slow gradual change. Whatever it is that marriage does, it changes you. It may be the obligation; it may be the responsibility. People become less sensitive to each other's needs. They do something because they have to, not because they want to. So I'd rather be the girlfriend than the wife. For some reason 'wife' is a bad word to me. So much is expected of you. It's a role, and if something doesn't turn out, it's your fault but I don't feel resentful or regretful. It was an experience. Today, I feel I'm a better person than I was 10 years ago, because I know a lot more, I've learned a lot".

"Life just kind of does things, you know. I can't change, and Elvis had his work and the things he had to do, and he can't change. One day you realize that it's going to be this way forever, so you have to make adjustments and when you know where you stand, you no longer have to please anybody but yourself. Then you can begin to live and have an identity without depending on someone else - no matter who that someone else may be'.

In West Germany, the 14-year old Priscilla would hang out at the Eagles Club, a place for eating and entertainment, Priscilla saying she'd often just listen to the juke box, while writing letters to her friends. One day, a handsome looking man, somewhere in his mid 20s approached her, whose name was Currie Grant. He asked Priscilla, 'How'd you like to meet Elvis Presley? My wife and I are good friends of his'.

Priscilla agreed, having worn a white and navy sailor dress on the night she was to meet Presley, who lived off base in Bad Nauheim. On the evening of Sunday, September 13th, 1959, Currie, his wife, and Priscilla drove for 40 minutes to get to Elvis' house. Nervous, Priscilla didn't speak much but when she arrived, entered the house then met Presley, he took a liking to her right away, seeming to be trying to impress Priscilla with his songs that he played her.

After that first night of meeting Elvis, Priscilla couldn't concentrate on school, but she told nobody that she'd met him, because she thought, "Who'd believe that just last night I was at Elvis' house?" Much was made of Priscilla having been only 14 when the pair were introduced, but she was mature for her age, with Presley being mindful of the implications of the situation.

Elvis wanted to see Priscilla again, who began visiting him regularly for 6 months, almost as if they were a couple. Priscilla thought of nothing but Presley, she cared for him, listened to him, and accompanied him, the pair being almost inseparable, until Elvis had to return to the US. Priscilla was photographed by the press at the airport when Presley left for America, with some of the photos ending up in Life magazine but there was surprisingly little other publicity about their relationship.

After Elvis was discharged from the Army, his only contact with Priscilla was over the phone and by mail, as 2 months shy of her 15th birthday, the blue-eyed brunette with the turned-up nose remained in West Germany. Within days there were reports that he was dating Nancy Sinatra, it being 3 weeks before Priscilla next heard Presley's voice, reassuring her that she was the only girl for him. Over the next two years she grew accustomed to the rumours and his denials, as well as the pain and frustration that came with loving the world's biggest heartthrob from a distance of over 3000 miles.

In a press conference on the day that he arrived back at Graceland, Elvis played down his relationship with 'the girl he left behind' but although he was dating Anita Wood and several actresses, he seemed to have reserved a special place in his heart for 'Cilla'. For the time being, Presley went along with Colonel Parker's belief that an all-consuming relationship would hurt his image and be bad for his career, as Priscilla patiently waited for their reunion.

During their conversations, Elvis would discuss his career, even his relationship with Anita Wood, leading Priscilla to wonder where she fit in, but he also insisted that he wanted her to visit Graceland. Cilla just had to hang on, which she did for almost 2 years, despite newspaper and magazine articles linking Presley to beauties including Juliet Prowse and Tuesday Weld.

Anita Wood: "... in early 1962, I was coming down the backstairs into the kitchen, when I heard Elvis say, 'I'm having the hardest time making up my mind between the two' ... I knew exactly what he was talking about and I had a lot of pride ... so I just marched my little self right down the stairs ... Elvis took me into the dining room where his dad was sitting at the table then we sat down at the table and I said, 'I'm gonna make that decision for you, I heard what you said and I'm leaving'.

I remember that I started crying, it was a very difficult decision to make. I must say that was probably the most difficult decision that I've ever made in my life. I have to say that. After having dated someone like Elvis for 5 years, and as close as we were for this to end but when I left, I knew there'd be no going back ... I said, 'I'm leaving', then I called Andy, my brother, to come to pick me up and we sat there and talked a little bit longer, but nobody could eat".

Then, one day during March 1962, after several months without contact, Presley called Priscilla out of the blue, inviting her to join him in Los Angeles. Stunned and overjoyed, she pointed out that, although her mother might be receptive to the idea, it would be nearly impossible to persuade her father, Captain Paul Beaulieu but it was a challenge Elvis seemed happy to accept.

While Priscilla prevailed upon her mother, Presley spoke with the Captain several times, finally winning him over by agreeing to a list of rules: the fortnight-long holiday wouldn't take place until Priscilla was out of school for the summer; Elvis would send her a first-class round-trip ticket; the Beaulieus would be provided with a comprehensive itinerary of her daily activities in Los Angeles; she would be chaperoned everywhere; she'd write to her parents every day; and at night she'd stay with his friends, George and Shirley Barris.

Priscilla arrived in Los Angeles in June then following a visit to Presley's house on Bellagio Road, she did stay at the Barris home -- for one night. The next afternoon, Elvis informed her that he'd planned a trip to Las Vegas then shortly after midnight she was sitting next to him in his luxury motor home on the way to Nevada. She circumvented the problem of her parents receiving letters each day by pre-writing a week's worth then asking Presley's butler to mail them from Los Angeles. Their next stop was the Sahara Hotel and Casino, where the King and his princess shared a suite.

During 12 blissful, fun-filled days and nights in Las Vegas, Elvis took Priscilla shopping, chose the clothes she should wear, while instructing her on how to style her hair and apply heavier makeup. Presley liked his women to wear plenty of eyeliner and mascara, Priscilla readily acceptingm his choices. Courtesy of an hairdresser at the hotel, her tresses were teased and twisted into a beehive style, with her eyes being heavily made up, the result being the apparent transformation of an innocent teen into a sophisticated siren.

Following her return to Germany, Priscilla had something to look forward to over the next 6 months: Christmas at Graceland. Elvis had invited her, so once again she had to persuade her parents but that request was nothing compared to what the Beaulieus were confronted with once the Christmas trip was over, when their darling daughter returned home: Presley wanted her to finish school in Memphis, calling Captain Beaulieu, to use all his powers of persuasion.

If Cilla moved to Memphis, he promised, she wouldn't live with him at Graceland but with Vernon and his wife in their house nearby. She'd be enrolled in the very best Catholic school, where he'd ensure that she'd graduate and she'd be cared for and chaperoned wherever she went. Not only did Elvis swear that he loved, needed, and respected Priscilla, but also insisted that he couldn't live without her. The Beaulieus were left with two painful alternatives: let Priscilla go, risking her being devastated if things didn't work out, or veto the proposed plan, being responsible for destroying her happiness. In the end, Elvis got his way, with Priscilla moving to Memphis.

While he was in Hollywood filming Fun in Acapulco, Elvis played host to Priscilla and her dad, winning over the senior Beaulieu with his charm and hospitality. After a few days, father and daughter flew to Memphis, where Captain Beaulieu and Vernon Presley enrolled Priscilla in the all-girl Immaculate Conception Cathedral High School then moved her into the home that Vernon shared with his 2nd wife, Dee.

However, once her father had returned to Germany, Priscilla seemed uncomfortable living with her future in-laws, soon spending more and more time with Elvis' grandmother at Graceland. Before long, for all intents and purposes she'd basically moved there. Vernon chauffeured Priscilla to and from school until she got her licence, when he agreed to let her drive Elvis' Lincoln Mark V.

He also provided her with pocket money to spend on clothes, petrol, and going to the movies, bowling alley, and Leonard's Drive-In with cousin Patsy, whose mother was Gladys's sister Clettes, and father was Vernon's brother Vester. Despite the company of Grandma Dodger, the maids, and the secretaries,

Priscilla often seemed very lonely waiting for Elvis to return from filming, one such movie being 'Viva Las Vegas'.

Priscilla: "Some stars want to meet other stars. Some stars have to hang out with other stars. Not Elvis. I can't remember him once telling the Colonel to arrange a meeting with anyone famous. He saw Hollywood as the home of phonies. He certainly felt out of place, which is why the minute the movie wrapped he was gone".

One memorable evening, the Colonel arranged for Elvis to meet 4 famous people but I believe it was the Beatles who were eager to meet Elvis, not the other way around. In fact, when John, Paul, Ringo and George walked in, Elvis was relaxing on the couch, looking at TV without the sound. He barely bothered to get up. Naturally he was curious about the Beatles. He respected them.

Mostly he respected the way they'd achieved their artistic freedom. He saw how they did whatever they liked to do. He appreciated their songs and especially their film 'A Hard Day's Night,' where their creativity and sense of fun came through so powerfully. 'Help!' was out or just about to be released. He also admired Bob Dylan and appreciated Dylan's serious songwriting".

Presley's love interest in the movie was non other than the 'Female Elvis', Ann-Margret... They were instantly attacted to each other, with a relationship developing which crushed Priscilla. She'd try to call Elvis to visit, but each time he'd delay it. Even after the film, reports were still everywhere. Cilla couldn't take it anymore, but Presley would threaten to have her go back to live with her parents if she protested, which is what happened one day, when she threw a vase at the wall. Elvis began packing her bags, telling Vernon to set up the next plane flight back to her folks, before apologizing saying, 'See..you needed this'.

One evening shortly before Christmas 1966, Presley went down on one knee in the bedroom at Graceland to propose to Cilla then slipped a ring on her finger. Bought from jeweler Harry Levitch, the ring featured a 3 1/2-carat diamond encircled by a row of smaller, detachable diamonds. Just over 7 years after their first meeting Elvis and Priscilla were married on Monday, May 1st, 1967.

Presley filmed 'Clambake' in Los Angeles while Colonel Parker made the wedding arrangements, the ceremony taking place at the Aladdin Hotel in Las Vegas, in the small 2nd-floor suite of the Colonel's friend, owner Milton Prell. The nuptials were presided over by Nevada Supreme Court Justice David Zenoff, taking under 10 minutes. In true Colonel Parker style, a press conference was held afterwards, followed by a breakfast reception for 100 guests, including many members of the press.

The newlyweds spent their honeymoon in Palm Springs, returning to Memphis after a couple of days where, on May 29th, they put their wedding attire back on, throwing a reception at Graceland for their relatives, friends, and employees, as well as a few lucky fans. Absent was bodyguard Red West, who refused to attend because he hadn't been invited to the actual wedding ceremony.

Under 2 months after the wedding, Elvis began work on 'Speedway' then on July 12th he made an announcement on the set that Priscilla was pregnant. Lisa Marie, was born on February 1st, 1968, Presley being a doting father to Lisa Marie. Until the end of his life Elvis adored Lisa Marie, spoiling her, showering her with jewels and gifts when she visited him, while rarely, if ever, disciplining her. As in many other aspects of his life, Presley's love for his daughter ran to excess.

Once, he flew her aboard his private jet so she could play in the snow then he rented the amusement park Libertyland on her birthday for Lisa Marie and her friends. Elvis bought her a golf cart and a pony, which he let her ride through the front door of Graceland. Priscilla stated in her autobiography that she and Presley kept their mutual affinity, relishing their joint role as parents. During one of their last phone conversations, Priscilla mused over the possibility that one day it might be their time again'.Yeah,' Elvis joked, 'when I'm 70 and you're 60. We'll both be so old, we'll look really silly, racing around in golf carts'.

Their divorce was finalized on October 9th, 1973, the two remaining friends, having held hands during the proceedings. Priscilla then opened a boutique, which she ran for 5 years before getting into modeling and acting. After signing with the William Morris Agency, Priscilla made her TV debut in 1980 as a co-host of the ABC series Those Amazing Animals with the legendary Burgess Meredith. Priscilla went on to portray the lead role of Jenna Wade on the TV soap opera Dallas from 1983 - 1988, starring as Jane Spencer, Jane Drebin in the third movie, with Leslie Nielsen in The Naked Gun film trilogy.

Priscilla, believed that part of her mission in life was to protect Presley's legacy, which led her to write her book Elvis and Me (1987), which she viewed as a response to Albert Goldman's vicious tome 'Elvis'. She didn't want Lisa to read Goldman's book then 'think that's what her father was'. Priscilla doesn't read all the books published on Presley, but she has a favourite: Peter Guralnick's Last Train to Memphis. "He really captured the whole mood, the whole time and the whole event of Elvis. I think he said it beautifully", she said.

After Elvis' death Priscilla took control of Elvis Presley Enterprises, building it into the organization it's become. Learning to deal with the business was a challenge, as there was no school for her, so she observed others, including Elvis' longtime manager Colonel Tom Parker, having learned by trial and error: "I learned a lot from the Colonel of what not to do. The challenge with the estate is to keep up the quality and maintain his legacy so it's always respected".

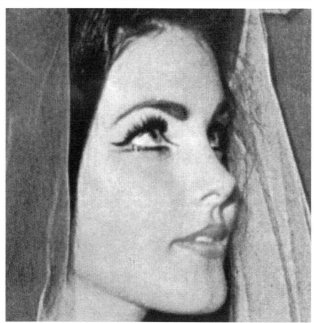

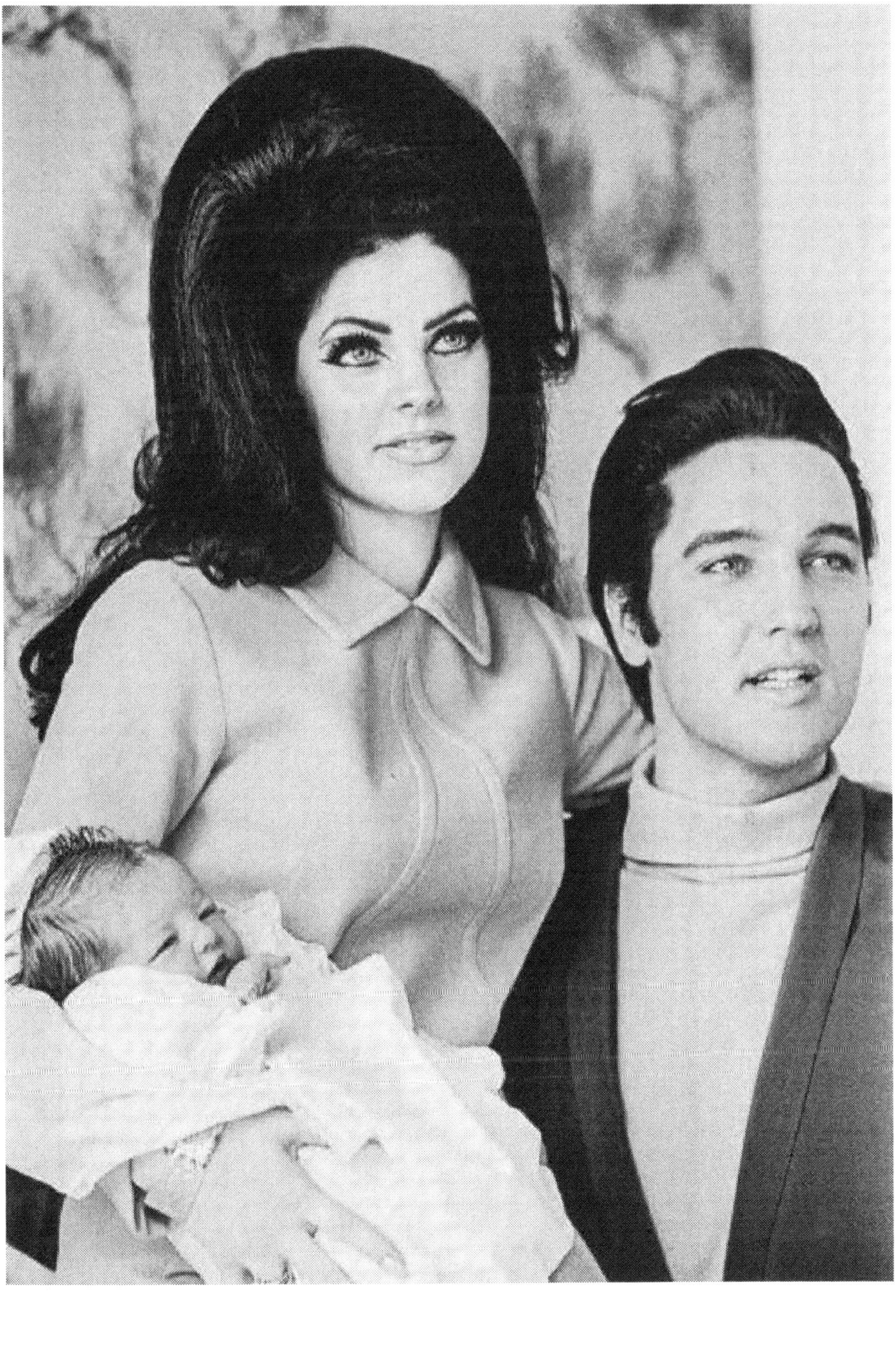

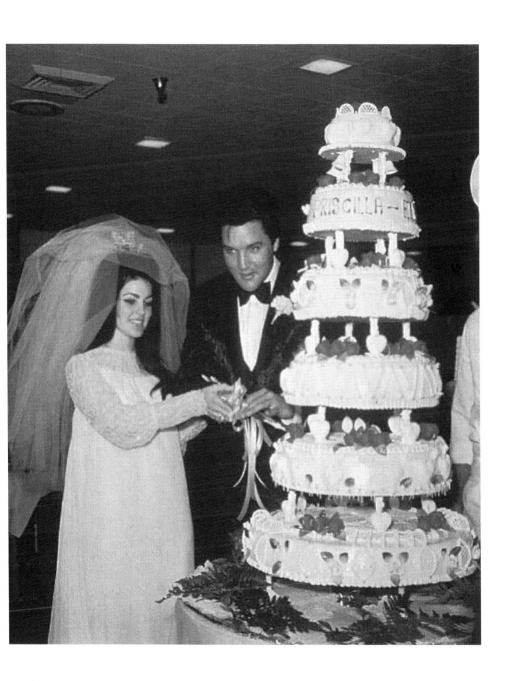

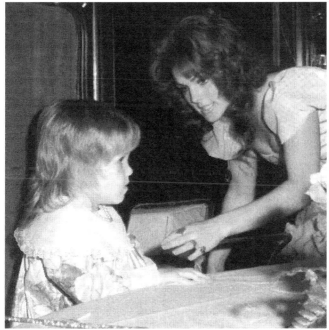

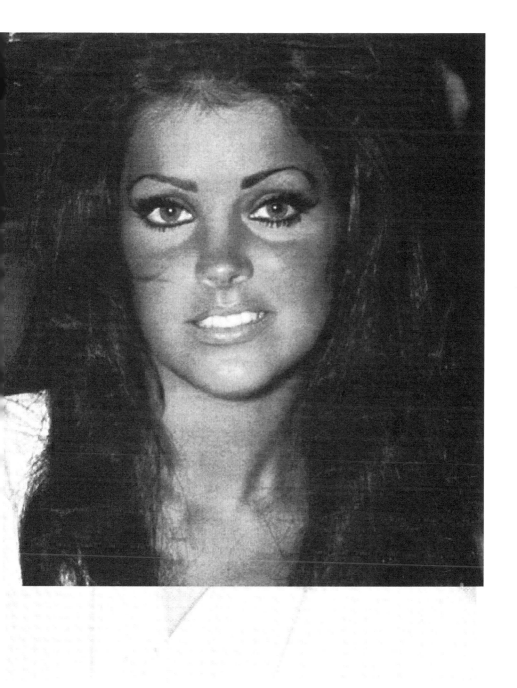

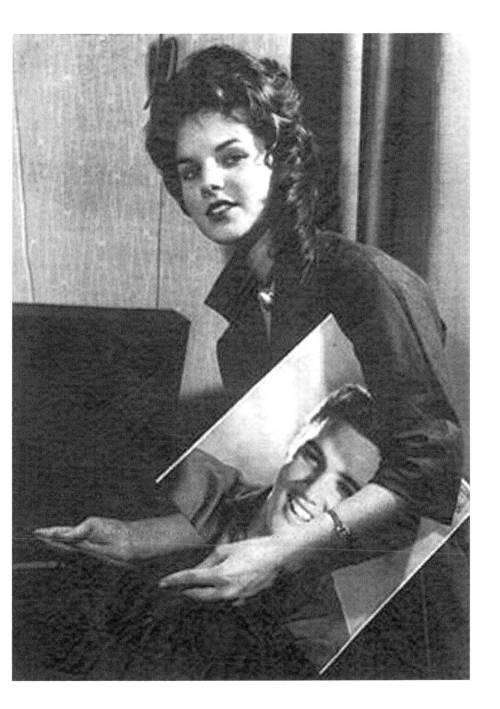

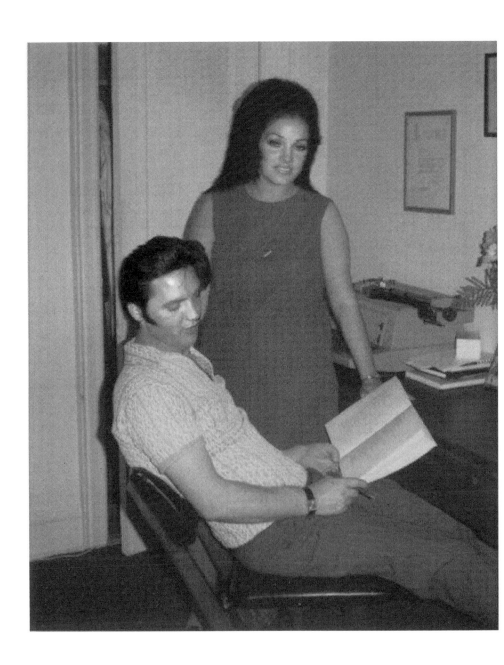

Printed in Great Britain
by Amazon